HEARTS AND FLOWERS

Feeling romantic? Rich burgundy and petal pink colors add a spark of passion to your decorating theme. These projects also make lovely gifts for an engagement party or wedding.

instructions on pages 22 - 23 and 26

MARCH

Luck of the Irish

It may be a wee bit of blarney, but the four-leaf clover has long been a symbol of good fortune. Add a touch of Irish charm to your festivities with a shower of shamrocks worked in lamb's wool or punch needle.

instructions on page 27

Pearl Cotton or Embroidery Floss

You can do punch needle embroidery with different types of threads. Using floss takes more time because you have to separate the strands each time you thread the punch needle. Pearl cotton is faster because you can work off of a spool so you only thread the punch needle when you start each color. However, pearl cotton is more costly to use than embroidery floss.

Hand-dyed pearl cotton is beautiful but is not colorfast; therefore, washing these projects is not recommended.

We used *Crescent Colours* and *DMC* embroidery floss as well as #5 & #8 pearl cotton from *Weeks Dye Works* and *DMC*. We used *DMC* Medicis wool thread on some of the projects in this book.

Basic Supplies for Wool:

Hand dyed wool fabric or felt
Poly-fil for pillows
Steam-A-Seam II fusible web
Sharp scissors
Craft & Applique Sheet
White chalk pencil and Black fine point pen for tracing

Basic Craft Supplies

Wood or paper mache boxes
Paint and Paintbrushes

Cardinals

Punch Needle Box and Table Topper

One of the first signs that Spring is coming is the return of Cardinals to their nesting sites.

Enjoy these bright red birds year-round in punch needle or soft wool.

instructions on pages 42 - 43

February

Heartfelt Love

Love is in the air! Celebrate your anniversary and Valentine's Day in style with these heartwarming designs.

instructions on pages 24 - 26

Spring Tulips

Grown with love and needing no watering, these gorgeous blooms are ready to grace any room in your home.

We made 2 tulips so you can see the difference in a single pattern that was punched in two different threads. It's amazing how different they look!

instructions on pages 28 - 29

May Baskets

April showers bring May flowers, and these baskets are brimming with beauty just in time for Mother's Day.

instructions on pages 20 - 21

In this book, you'll find a fabulous selection of designs for punch needle projects as well as lovely complementary wool applique patterns that celebrate everyone's favorite times of the year.

JUNE

Honeyed Summer Flowers

Every season nature strives to outdo herself, bringing luxurious colors and lustrous tones to her creations. Interpret the beauty of a summer's day with these golden designs.

instructions on pages 32 - 33

Those Lazy Days of Summer

Let the sun shine in! Need to brighten your day or cheer someone you care about? Send them a sunflower stitched with love in punch needle or fun appliques.

instructions on pages 30 - 31

Fruits of the Season

August

Enjoy the fruits of the season every day of the year. These delicious creations coordinate with any kitchen or dining decor.

instructions on page 32

SEPTEMBER

HALCYON DAYS

There is just a little nip in the air and the wind has shifted out of the north. Fall is coming! These projects are for everyone who loves leaping into a pile of leaves or treasures the colors of maple and oak after the first frost.

instructions on pages 34 - 35

Harvest Time

Fall comes dressed in her favorite colors - orange, gold, red, pumpkin and brown. This rich color combination is a pleasure we enjoy at harvest time. Immerse yourself in nature's choice with these fabulous fall projects.

instructions on pages 46 & 48

Give Thanks

The key to a happy life is a grateful heart. Express the sentiments of an American holiday with easy to applique designs and pretty punch needle.

instructions on pages 36 - 37

Happy Holly Days

Holly remains green through the winter making it a wonderful motif for decorating the season of joy, hope, love, and peace.

instructions on pages 38 - 39

Christmas Poinsettias

Ah, Christmas! The hot cocoa steams, the yule log roars, and the poinsettias look gorgeous on the dining table. Sprinkle the holiday spirit throughout the house with a collection of hand made home decor.

instructions on pages 40 - 41

O Christmas Tree

December

Deck your halls with simple gifts and old world style. The Christmas star shines brighter against the beauty of these unadorned branches.

instructions on pages 44 - 45

Antique Jar Lids

Add some country spice to your decor all year long with punch needle displayed in antique jar lids - perfect for hanging in the kitchen.

instructions on pages 46-47

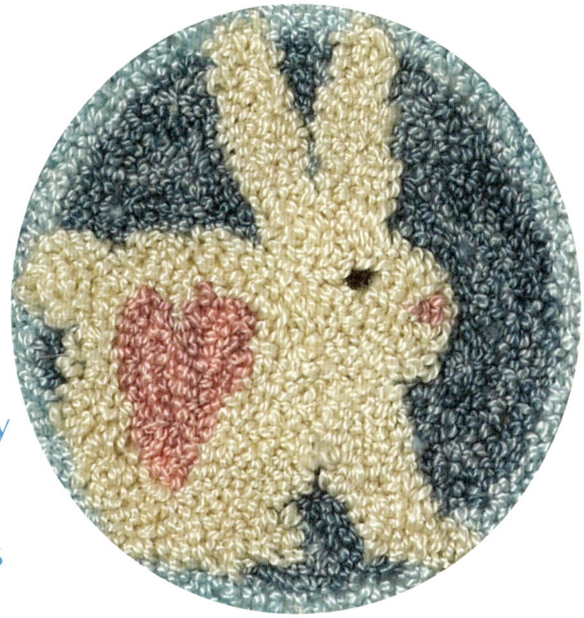

Our newest collection will inspire your artistry and encourage you to express your creativity.

We hope you enjoy these projects as much as we have enjoyed bringing them to you.

Basic Directions for Punch Needle Embroidery

Materials:

Punch Needle with threader
Weaver's Cloth
Pearl cotton or embroidery floss
Light table for tracing designs
Locking type hoop
Small sharp scissors

Preparing a Punch Needle Project:

Cut Weaver's cloth 3" larger than the final project will be.

Punch needle is worked from the back, so the design is printed in reverse. Using tracing paper, trace the pattern and then transfer the Punch Needle design to the Weaver's cloth using a light table. Place the pattern on the light table. Center the Weaver's cloth over the pattern, and trace the pattern onto the Weaver's cloth using a fine point pen.

Threading the Needle:

There are 4 steps to threading the needle.

1. Insert threader into the punch from the needle tip.

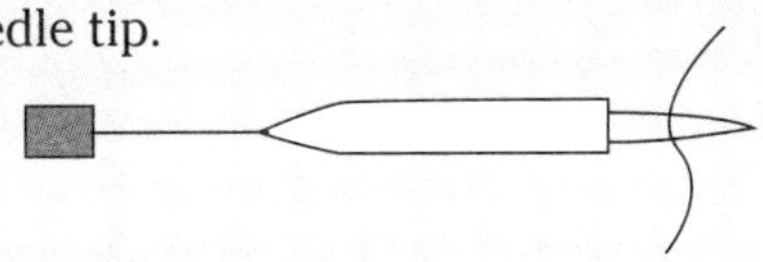

2. Drop the thread into the threader and pull back through the shaft.

3. Insert threader into the back of the eye of the needle.

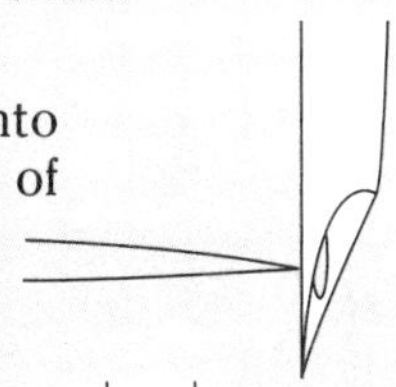

4. Drop thread into eye of the threader and pull back.

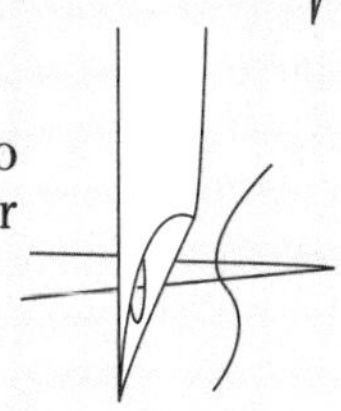

Position Weaver's cloth in a hoop. Follow the manufacturer's instructions for using your needle tool.

Refer to the color photos of each project to determine color placement.

Setting the Depth:

The higher the setting, the taller the loop. Most of our designs are punched at the lowest setting. Each brand of punch needle is different. Check your manual before beginning.

Punching:

Unroll the pearl cotton or untwine the floss before you thread the needle. Practice a straight row on a scrap of fabric. Keep the fabric pulled very tight in the hoop, in all directions, or your project may get distorted. Hold the hoop at an angle. Punch quickly, all the way down, pull up the tip of the needle just above the fabric.

You may hear a click when the needle brushes past the fabric. Move over and punch down again. The loops should be consistent, all the same size across. Don't punch too tightly. Leave a space the thickness of the thread you are using. If not, try again.

You'll quickly develop a rhythm.

Keep the open end of the needle (front) aimed towards the direction you are punching. The tail of the thread should follow .

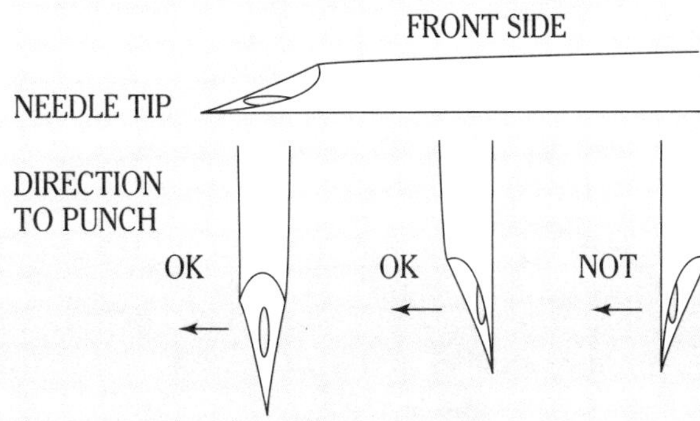

Finishing Projects

1. Trim the fabric leaving a ½" border.
2. Fold excess border fabric to the back so it does not show.
3. Hand baste excess fabric to the back.

Basic Instructions for Wool Embroidery

TIP: Wool can be appliqued with or without fusible web.

With Fusible Web:

1. Trace the pattern pieces in reverse onto the fusible web paper and roughly cut apart each piece.
2. Peel paper backing off of the fusible web and press to the back of the wool following manufacturer's instructions.
3. Cool and cut out each piece.
4. Peel off paper backing and position each piece on the wool background.
5. Fuse following manufacturer's instructions.
6. Blanket stitch around each wool piece.

Without Fusible Web:

1. Trace each pattern piece onto a plastic template and cut out. Use the templates to trace the wool pieces and cut each piece out.
2. Position and pin to the backing fabric.
3. Blanket stitch around each wool piece.

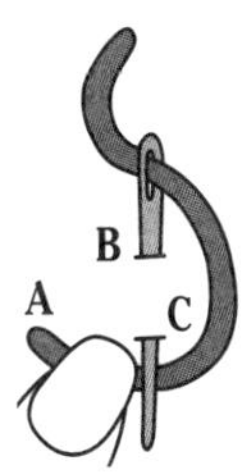

Blanket Stitch

Come up at A, hold the thread down with your thumb, go down at B. Come back up at C with the needle tip over the thread. Pull the stitch into place. Repeat, outlining with the bottom legs of the stitch. Use this stitch to edge fabrics.

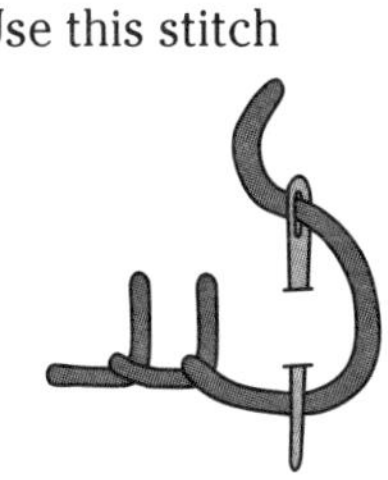

Wool Design

Vase of Flowers

photo on page 8

SIZE: Punch needle: 3½" x 3⅝"
Frame: 5" x 7"

MATERIALS:

Weeks Dye Works #8 pearl cotton:
- Romance #2274 for flowers and border rows
- Ivy #2198 for leaves
- Schneckley #1223 for vase
- 2 Fawn #1111 for background

7" x 7" Weaver's cloth
3 buttons
5" x 7" *Weeks Dye Works* Green wool for framing
5" x 7" frame
Fabric glue

INSTRUCTIONS:

Punch in the following order: Flowers • Leaves • Vase • Background • 2 rows of border
See page 19 for Finishing instructions.
Sew a button to the center of each flower.
Adhere Green wool to frame mat for background.
Adhere finished punch needle project to center of frame.

Flower Basket Wool Pillow

SIZE: 12½" x 12½" photo on page 8

MATERIALS:

Weeks Dye Works wool:
- 13" x 13" Red Pear #1332 for top
- 3" x 9" Red Pear #1332 for flowers
- 3" x 6" Collards #1227 for leaves

National Nonwovens wool felt:
- 13" x 13" Black for back
- 10" diameter Black circle
- 5" x 7" Light Tan for vertical stripes on basket
- 8" x 10" Camel for horizontal stripes on basket and handle

#5 pearl cotton (Green, Pink)
Steam-A-Seam II fusible web
Craft & Applique sheet
Clear template plastic
Poly-fil stuffing

INSTRUCTIONS:

1. Back the Tan and Camel felt with fusible web.
2. From the Tan felt, cut 5 strips, 1" x 4"
3. From the Camel felt, cut 4 strips, 1" x 7"
4. Remove the paper backing from the fusible web.
5. Leaving ½" between the Light Tan vertical strips, weave the Tan and Camel together, over and under. Place weaving on the Craft & Applique sheet. Fuse following manufacturer's instructions. Let cool. Peel off.
6. Trace the basket pattern onto clear plastic template and cut out.
7. Lay the pattern on top of the wool felt and cut out the basket shape.
8. Press the handle and basket onto the Black circle.
9. Cut out the flowers and leaves.
10. Sew leaves in place with 1 or 2 stitches at the base of each leaf.
11. Attach the flowers with a cluster of Gold French Knots in the center of each.
12. Position the Black circle in the center of the Pink pillow top. Blanket stitch in place with Pink pearl cotton.
13. With right sides together, sew a ¼" seam all the way around pillow, leaving 6" open for turning.
14. Turn right side out. Stuff with Poly-fil and hand stitch the opening closed.
15. Blanket stitch all the way around the seam using Green pearl cotton.

Basket of Flowers

photo on page 8

SIZE: Punch needle: 3⅛" x 3½"
Frame: 5" x 5"

MATERIALS:

Weeks Dye Works #5 pearl cotton:
- Camellia #2276 for flowers
- Scuppermong#2196 for leaves
- Beige #1106 for basket
- 2 Onyx #1304 for background

DMC #5 pearl cotton Gold for French Knots
7" x 7" Weaver's cloth
5" x 5" *Weeks Dye Works* Dark Pink wool for framing
5" x 5" frame
Fabric glue

INSTRUCTIONS:

Punch in the following order: Flowers • Leaves • Basket • Background
Make a Gold French Knot on the center of each flower.
See page 19 for Finishing instructions.
Adhere Dark Pink wool to frame mat for background.
Adhere finished punch needle project to center of frame.

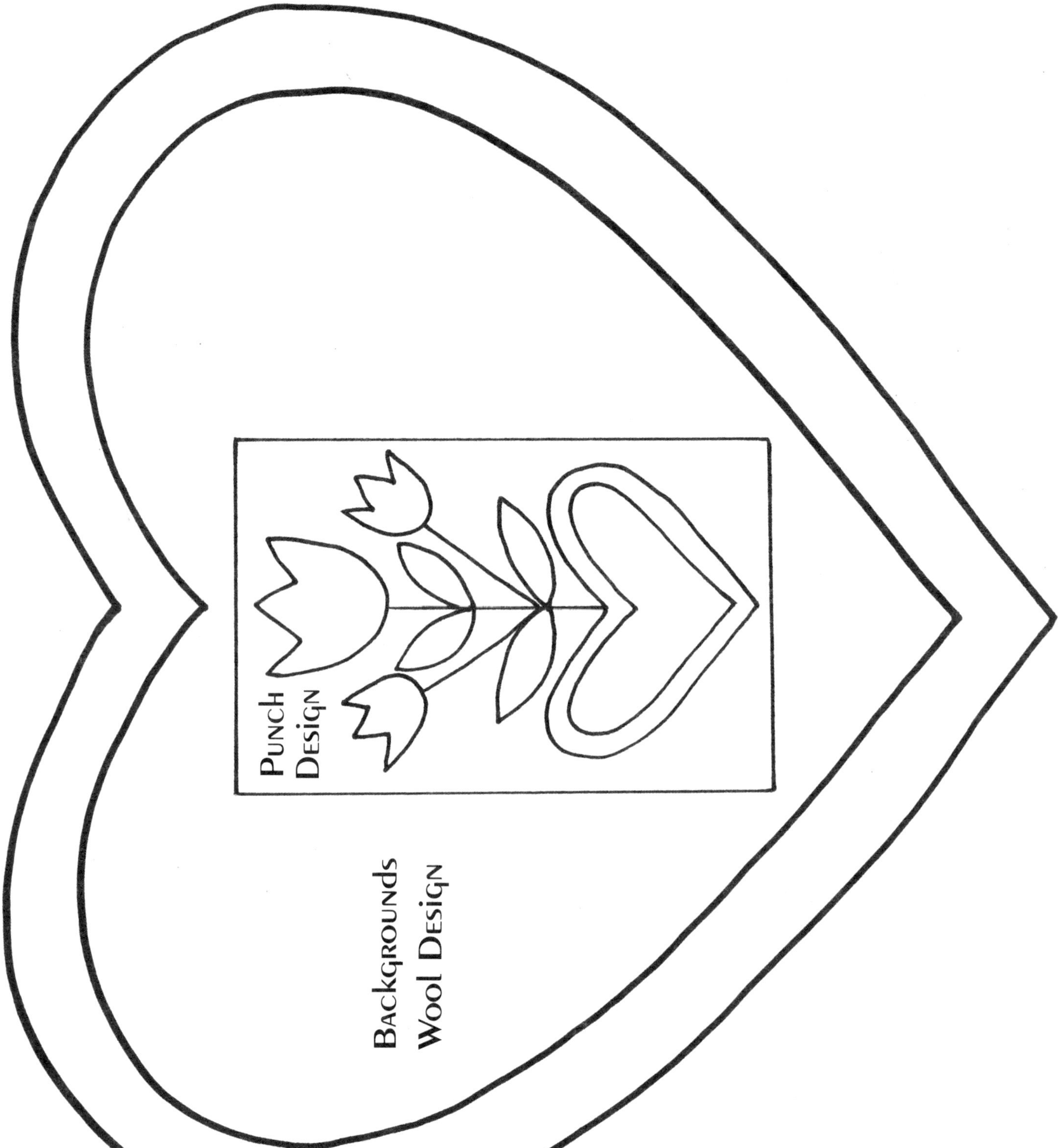

Heart Mug Rug

photo on page 5
SIZE: Punch needle: 2" x 4"
Heart: 7½" x 8¼"

MATERIALS:
Weeks Dye Works wool:
7" x 8" Peony #2271 HB for small heart
8" x 9" hand-dyed Red for large heart
Weeks Dye Works #8 pearl cotton:
Sweetheart Rose #2279 for large tulip and inner heart
Garnet #2264 for small tulips, outer heart and border
Scuppermong #2196 for leaves
3 Beige #1101 for background
DMC #8 pearl cotton, Deep Maroon #902 for Blanket stitching
5" x 7" Weaver's cloth

INSTRUCTIONS:
Punch in the following order: Large tulip and inner heart • Small tulips and outer heart • Leaves • Background • 1 row on the border using Garnet
See page 19 for finishing instructions.

1. Cut out hearts using pattern.
2. Lay the small heart on the large one, centered.
3. Using Deep Maroon pearl cotton, Blanket stitch small heart in place, then Blanket stitch around the large heart.
4. Hand stitch the finished punch needle project to the center.

Heart

photo on page 5

SIZE: 9" x 12½"

MATERIALS:

Weeks Dye Works hand-dyed wool:

- 9" x 18" Deep Red for the background, large heart, and tulips
- 4" x 8" Mauve for small heart and 1 tulip
- 3" x 6" Green for leaves
- 7" x 10¼" Snow Cream #1096

DMC #5 pearl cotton (Green, White)

INSTRUCTIONS:

1. Cut Dark Red background 9" x 12½".
2. Cut out hearts, leaves and flowers.
3. Position pieces on the Snow Cream wool. Whipstitch in place.
4. Draw stems and stitch using Green pearl cotton.
5. Lay the appliqued wool on the background. Straight stitch all the way around using White pearl cotton.

Wool Design

Love Table Mat

photo on page 4
SIZE: $10\frac{1}{2}$" x $12\frac{1}{4}$"

MATERIALS:
Weeks Dye Works wool:
- $10\frac{1}{2}$" x $12\frac{1}{4}$" Merlot #1334 for background
- $8\frac{3}{4}$" x $10\frac{1}{2}$" Dark Mauve
- 3" x $10\frac{1}{2}$" Lighter Pink
- 4" x 8" Dark Red for letters and heart
- 5" x 5" White for heart

Matching #8 pearl cotton for Blanket stitching

INSTRUCTIONS:
1. Center Pink wool on the Dark Mauve wool. Whipstitch in place.
2. Cut out letters and hearts. Whipstitch in place.
3. Lay appliqued piece on Merlot background. Blanket stitch all the way around.
4. Blanket stitch all the way around the background using matching pearl cotton.

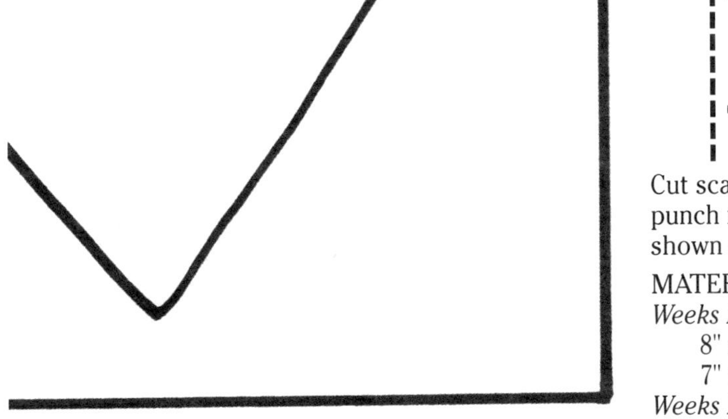

Cut scallop edges on fold. Sew Love punch needle panel to backgrounds as shown on pattern and diagram at right.

MATERIALS:
Weeks Dye Works wool:
8" x 8" hand-dyed Mauve for outer background
7" x 7" Bordeaux #1339 for inner background
Weeks Dye Works #5 pearl cotton:
Lancaster Red #1333 for letters and heart
Snowflake #4125 for heart
Chablis #1139 for center background

See page 19 for finishing instructions.

1. Cut out inner and outer backgrounds using pattern.
2. Blanket stitch around outer background with Dark Mauve pearl cotton.
3. Center inner background on outer. Blanket stitch in place.
4. Hand stitch the finished punch needle project to the center.

Love Mug Rug

photo on page 4

SIZE: Punch needle: 3" x 4"
Mug Rug: 7½" x 7½"

Punch Design

Teddy Bear

photo on page 4

SIZE:

Punch needle: 3¾" x 4½" oval

Frame: 5" x 7" oval

MATERIALS:

Weeks Dye Works #5 pearl cotton:
- Hibiscus #2278 for heart and bow tie
- Chestnut #1269 for outline of bear, nose and inner ears
- 2 Cocoa #1233 for bear body
- 2 Fawn #1111 for background

7" x 7½" Weaver's cloth

5" x 7" *Weeks Dye Works* Mauve wool for framing

5" x 7" oval frame

Fabric glue

INSTRUCTIONS:

Punch in the following order: Heart and bow tie • Outline of the bear, nose and inner ears • Bear's body • Background

See page 19 for Finishing instructions.

Glue Mauve wool to frame mat for background.

Glue finished punch needle to center of frame.

Punch Design

Tip: Before beginning the Posey's Altoid Tin, your fabric will stretch one way or the other when stretching in a hoop. Using the altoid tin as your pattern, make sure the design does not overhang the tin. Use a pen to draw the lines closer in if necessary.

Posey's Altoid Tin

photo on page 5

SIZE: Punch needle: 2½" x 3¾"

Tin: 2½" x 3¾" x 1" tall

MATERIALS:

DMC #8 pearl cotton:
- Green #3346 for leaves and stems
- Red #815 for flower centers

Weeks Dye Works #8 pearl cotton:
- Sweetheart Rose #2279 for flower petals
- 3 Beige #1106 for background

5½" x 7" Weaver's cloth

Hot glue gun

INSTRUCTIONS:

Punch in the following order: Stems and leaves • Centers of the flowers 3 times • Flower petals • Background

See page 19 for Finishing instructions.

Hot glue the finished piece to the top of an altoid tin.

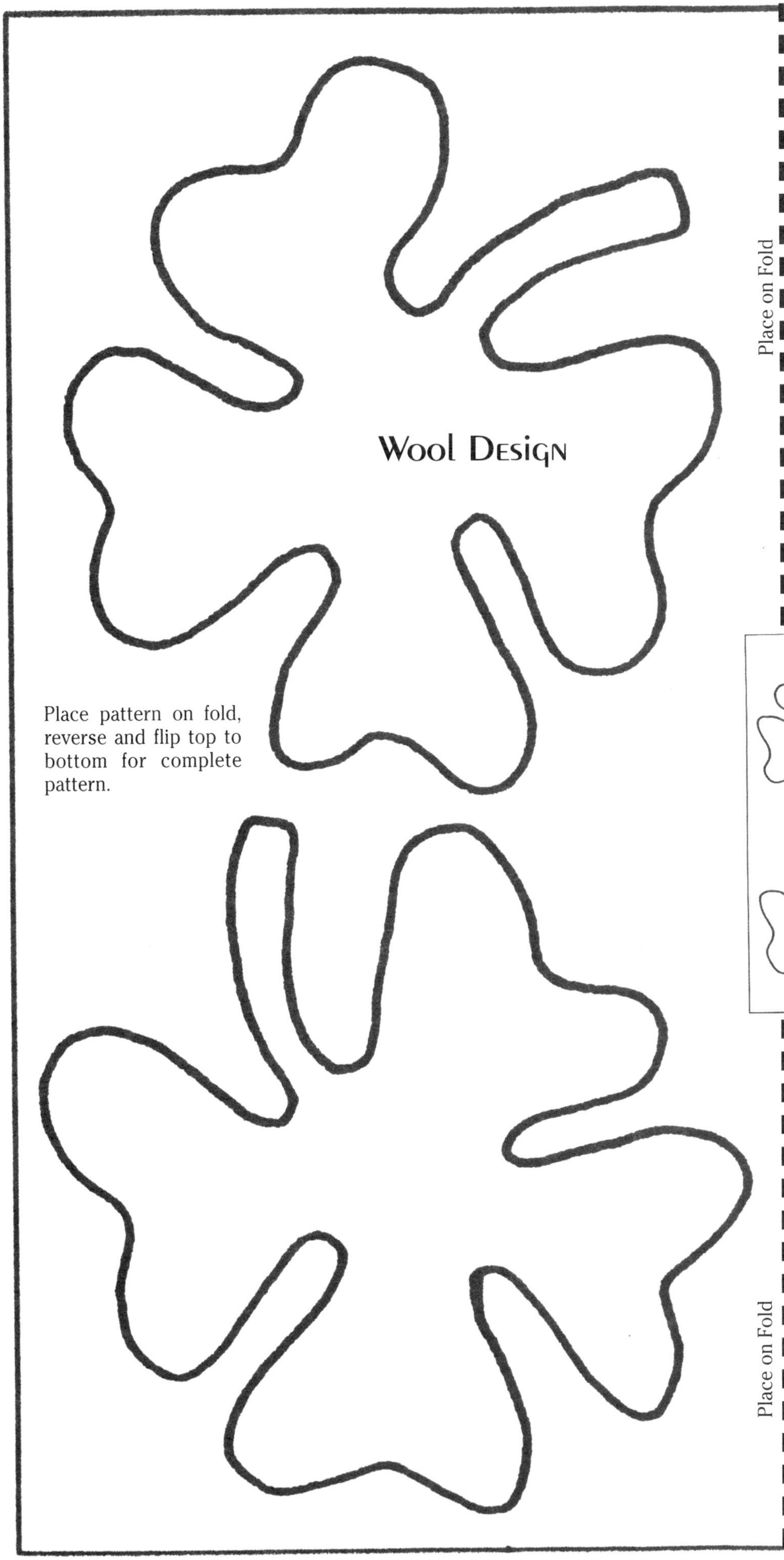

Shamrock Wool Pillow

photo on page 6

SIZE: 13" x 13"

MATERIALS:

Weeks Dye Works wool:
- Two 14" x 14" Collards HB #1227 for pillow
- 10" x 10" Collards HB #1227 for shamrocks
- 10½" x 10½" Snow Cream #1096 for background

Poly-fil stuffing

INSTRUCTIONS:

1. Cut out 4 shamrocks. Position on Snow Cream background. Whipstitch in place.
2. Position appliqued piece on pillow top. Straight stitch around the outer edge.
3. With right sides together, sew pillow with a ¼" seam all the way around, leaving 6" open for turning.
4. Turn right side out. Stuff with Poly-fil. Hand-stitch the opening closed.

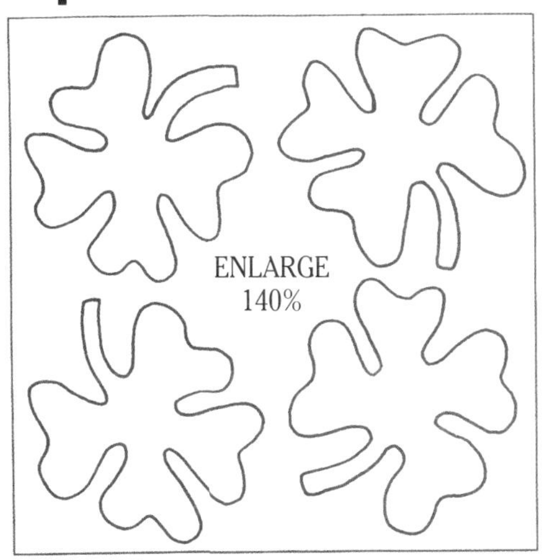

Enlarge 140%

Shamrock Box

photo on page 6

SIZE: Punch needle: 3½" x 3½"
Box: 4" x 4" x 4" tall

MATERIALS:

Weeks Dye Works #5 pearl cotton:
- Angel Hair #1109 for background
- Hunter #2156 for shamrocks

6" x 6" Weaver's cloth

4" x 4" x 4" paper mache box

Hot glue gun

INSTRUCTIONS:

Punch in the following order:
Shamrocks • Background

Paint box Dark Green. Let dry.

See page 19 for Finishing instructions.

Hot glue finished piece to box.

Tulips in Wool

photo on page 7

SIZE: Punch needle: 2¾" x 5"
Frame: 5" x 7"

MATERIALS:

DMC Medicis wool thread:
- Purple #8895 for tulips and curliques
- Dark Green #8403 for stem and inner border
- Green #8418 for leaves and outer border
- Ecru for background

6" x 8" Weaver's cloth

5" x 7" *Weeks Dye Works* Purple wool for framing

5" x 7" frame

Fabric glue

INSTRUCTIONS:

Punch in the following order: Purple tulips • Purple curliques • Dark Green stems • A row of Dark Green border • Green leaves • Several rows of Green outer border • Ecru background

See page 19 for finishing instructions.

Adhere Purple wool to frame mat for background.

Adhere the finished punch needle to center of frame.

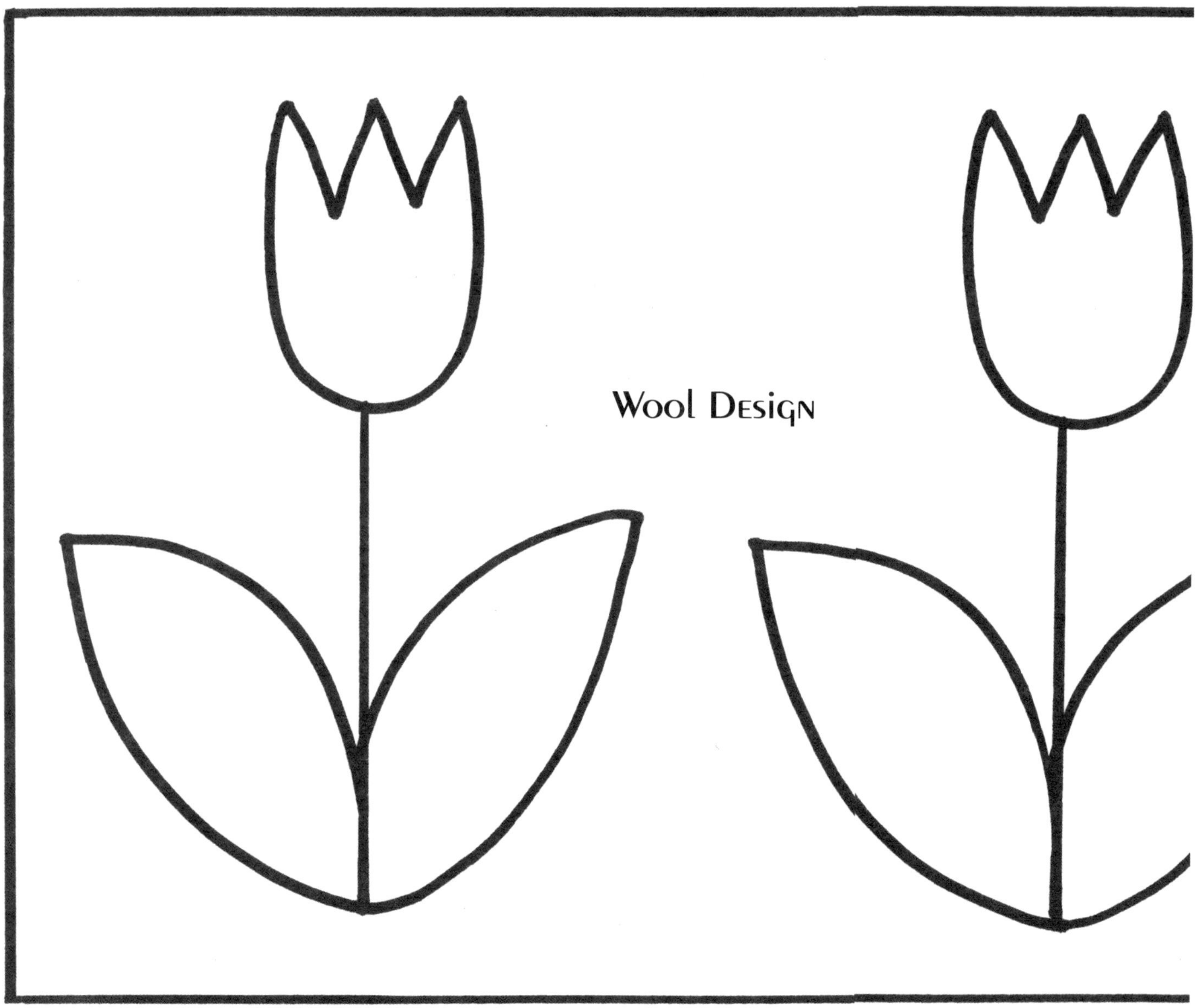

Tulips in Pearl Cotton

photo on page 7

SIZE: Punch needle: 2¾" x 5"
Frame: 5" x 7"

MATERIALS:

Weeks Dye Works #5 pearl cotton:
- Peoria Purple #2333 for flowers
- Juniper #2158 for stems, curliques and inner border
- Scuppermong #2196 for leaves and outer border
- 3 Light Khaki #1101 for background

6" x 8" Weaver's cloth
5" x 7" *Weeks Dye Works* Purple wool for framing
5" x 7" frame
Fabric glue

INSTRUCTIONS:

Punch in the following order: Purple tulips • Purple curliques • Dark Green stems • A row of Dark Green border • Green leaves • Several rows of Green outer border • Ecru background

See page 19 for finishing instructions.

Adhere Purple wool to frame mat for background.
Adhere finished punch needle to center of frame.

Tulips Table Runner

photo on page 7

SIZE: 16½" x 24"

MATERIALS:

Weeks Dye Works wool:
- 18½" x 24" Purple Rain #2338 HT for outer background and tulips
- 14½" x 22" Angel hair #1109 for inner background
- 4" x 12" Collards #1227 HB for leaves

DMC pearl cotton #5 Green #935 for stems and Blanket stitching

INSTRUCTIONS:

1. Cut outer background 16½" x 24".
2. Cut out 6 tulips and 6 leaves.
3. Position the flowers across each end of the Angel Hair inner background, ¾" from the edge.
4. Whipstitch the tulips and leaves in place.
5. Draw a line for the stems between the tulips and leaves. Stem stitch with Green pearl.
6. Lay appliqued top over Purple background.
7. Using Green pearl cotton, Blanket stitch around the edge of appliqued piece and around background.

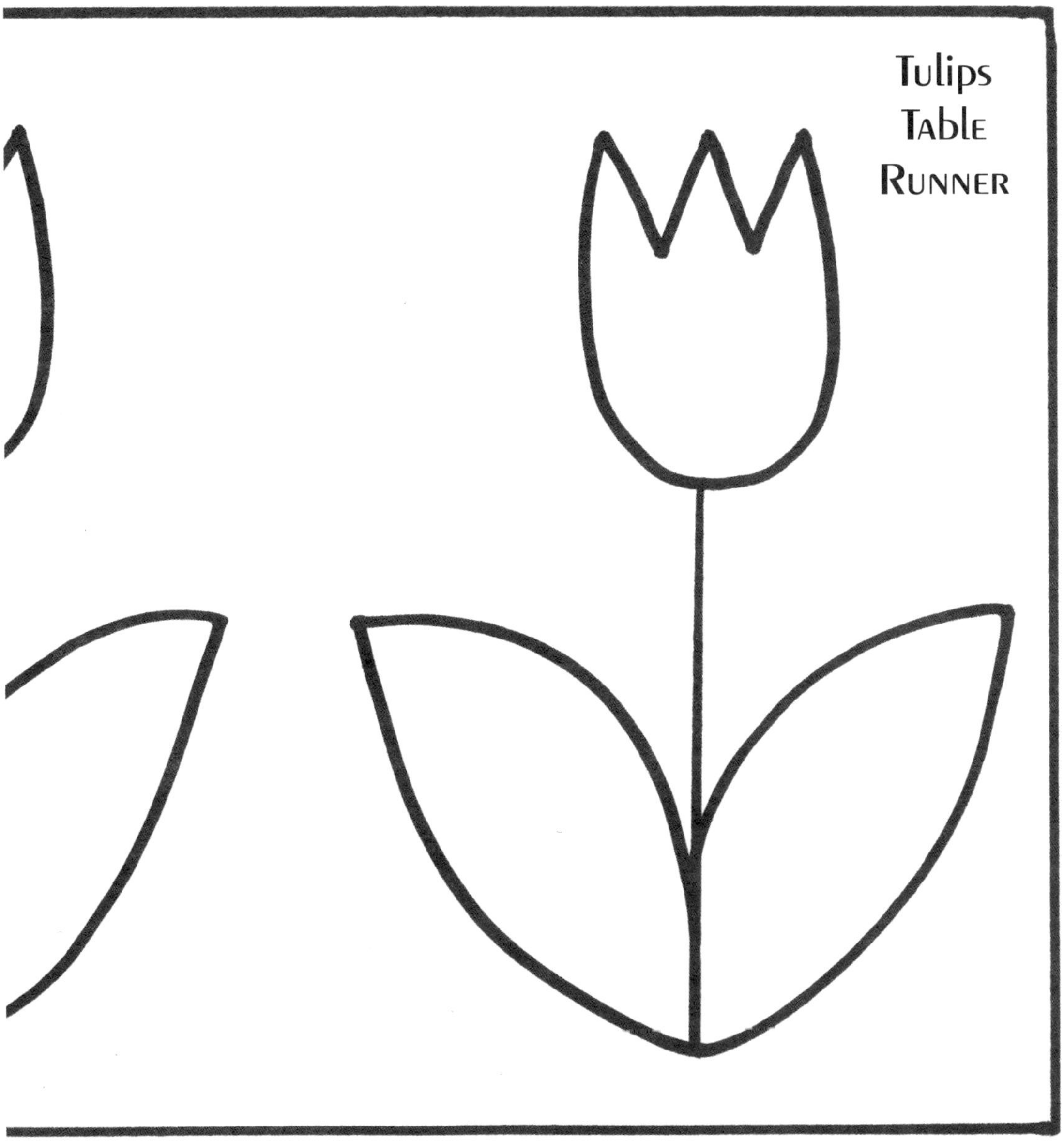

We made 2 tulips so you can see the difference in a single pattern that was punched in two different threads. It's amazing how different they look!

Sunflowers Table Mat

photo on page 10

SIZE: 10½" x 14½"

MATERIALS:

Weeks Dye Works hand-dyed wool:

- 10½" x 14½" Tan for background
- 8½" x 12½" Parchment #1110 HT for inner background
- Two 2½" x 8½" Tan rectangles
- 7" x 14" Mustard #1224a for sunflower
- 3" x 6" Chestnut #1269 for flower centers
- 3" x 5" Collards #1227 for leaf

Brown #5 pearl cotton

INSTRUCTIONS:

1. Cut out all pieces.
2. Position all pieces on the inner background. Whipstitch in place.
3. Draw the stems and stitch using Brown pearl cotton.
4. Straight stitch the appliqued top to the Tan background with Brown pearl cotton.
5. Blanket stitch around the outer edge with Brown pearl cotton.

Wool Design

Enlarge pattern 125%

Sunflowers Penny Rug

photo on page 10

SIZE: Punch needle: 3" x 4½"
Penny Rug: 8" x 9¾"

MATERIALS:

Weeks Dye Works wool:
- 8" x 10" Collards #1277 for scalloped background
- 9" x 9" Mustard #1224 for center background and circles

Weeks Dye Works #5 pearl cotton:
- Caper #1266 for flower centers
- 2 Gold #2221 for flower petals
- Ivy #2198 for leaves and stems
- 2 Light Khaki #1101 for center, top, and bottom background
- Beige #1106 for 2 remaining backgrounds

DMC #8 pearl cotton
- Gold #783
- Green #3345

6" x 8" Weaver's cloth

INSTRUCTIONS:

Punch in the following order: Flower centers • Flower petals • Leaves and stems • Center, top and bottom backgrounds • Remaining 2 backgrounds

See page 19 for Finishing instructions.

1. Using pattern, cut 1 scalloped background from Collards wool.
2. From Mustard wool, cut 1 rectangle 5¼" x 6¾" and 14 circles 1" diameter.
3. Blanket stitch the Mustard rectangle and circles in place with Gold pearl cotton.
4. Blanket stitch around the scalloped edge using Green pearl cotton.
5. Hand stitch the finished punch needle project to the center.

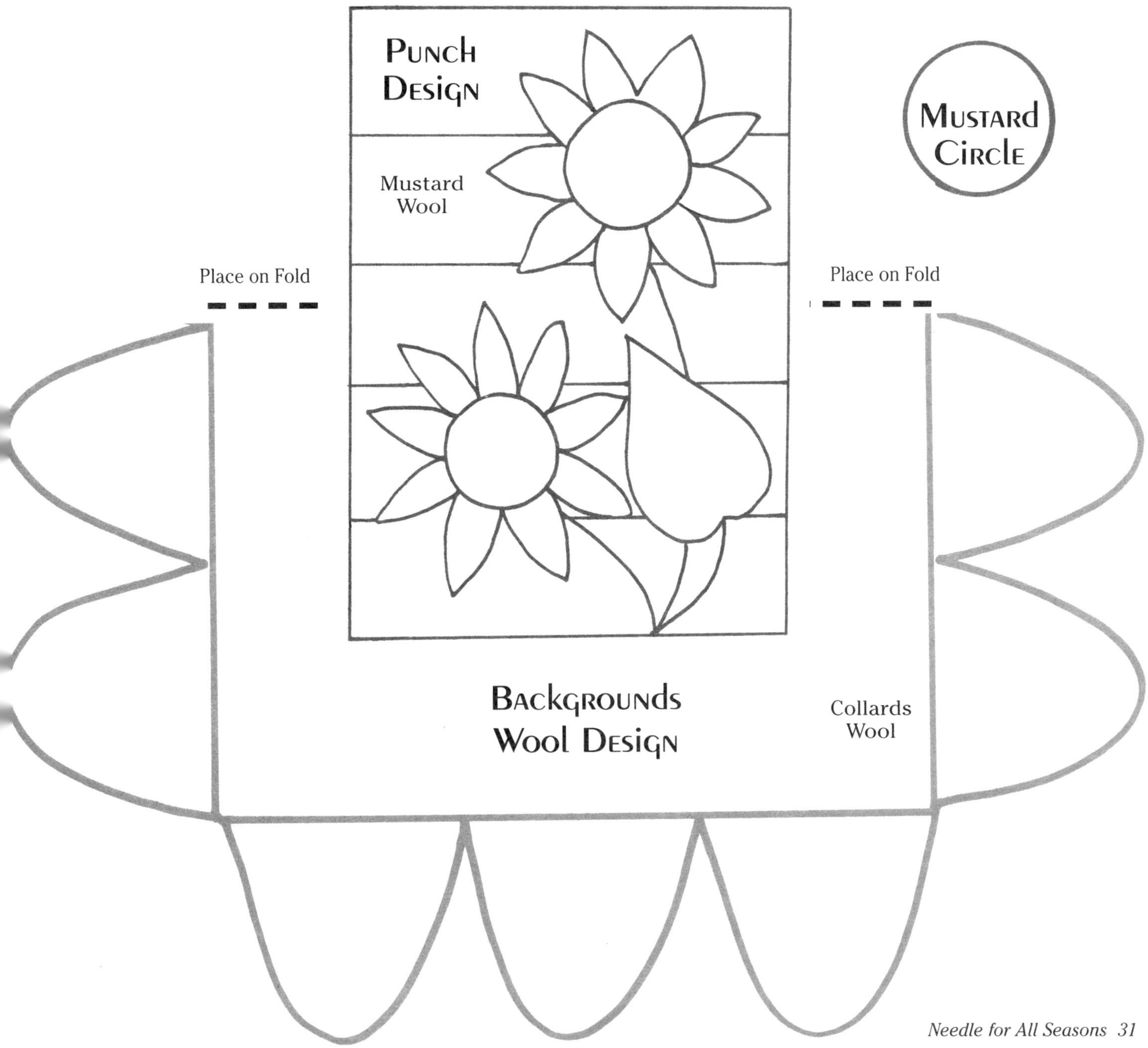

Punch Design

Daisy Box

photo on page 9

SIZE: Punch needle:
2¾" diameter
Box: 3" x 3" x 1½" tall

MATERIALS:

Weeks Dye Works #8 pearl cotton:
Whiskey #2219 for background

DMC #8 pearl cotton Blanc for flower

6" x 6" Weaver's cloth

⅜" Gold button

3" x 3" x 1½" paper mache box

Hot glue gun

INSTRUCTIONS:

Punch in the following order:
Flowers • Background

Sew a button on the center.

See page 19 for Finishing instructions.

Glue finished piece to box.

Apples Box

photo on page 11

SIZE: Punch needle: 2½" x 4¾"
Box: 4¼" x 6¾" x 2" tall
(We used a wooden cigar box.)

MATERIALS:

Weeks Dye Works #8 pearl cotton:
Chestnut #1269 for stems
Scuppermong #2196 for leaves and outer border
2 Garnet #2264 for apples and inner border
2 Beige #1106 for background

6" x 8" Weaver's cloth

4¼" x 6¾" x 2" tall wood box

Hot glue gun

INSTRUCTIONS:

Punch in the following order: Stems • Leaves • Apples • 1 Garnet row on the inner border • Background • 3 Scuppermong rows on the border

See page 19 for Finishing instructions.

Glue finished project to box.

Watermelon

photo on page 11

SIZE: Punch needle: 2" x 4"
5" x 7" frame

MATERIALS:

Weeks Dye Works 3 strands floss
Kohl #3900 for seeds
Blue Spruce #1276 for rind
Lancaster Red #1333 for Darker section on lower melon
Romance #2274 for Lighter section on melon
3 Fawn #1111 for background

5" x 7" Weaver's cloth

5" x 7" *Weeks Dye Works* Green wool for frameing

5" x 7" wood frame

Fabric glue

INSTRUCTIONS:

Punch in the following order: Seeds • Rind • Darker section of lower watermelon • Lighter section of upper watermelon • Background.

See page 19 for Finishing instructions.

Glue Green wool to frame mat for background.

Glue finished piece to center of the frame.

Strawberry Basket

photo on page 11

SIZE: Punch needle: 3⅜" diameter
Basket: 3¾" x 3¾" x 2¼" tall not including handle

MATERIALS:

DMC #8 pearl cotton:
Green #937 for leaves and stems
Red #815 for strawberries
Ecru for background

Weeks Dye Works #8 pearl cotton:
Deep Sea #2104 for bowl

7" x 7" Weaver's cloth

3¾" x 3¾" x 2¼" basket

Dark Brown stain

Hot glue gun

INSTRUCTIONS:

Punch in the following order: Stems and leaves • Strawberries • Bowl • Background

Stain the basket Dark Brown. Let dry.

Hot glue the finished punch needle project to the lid.

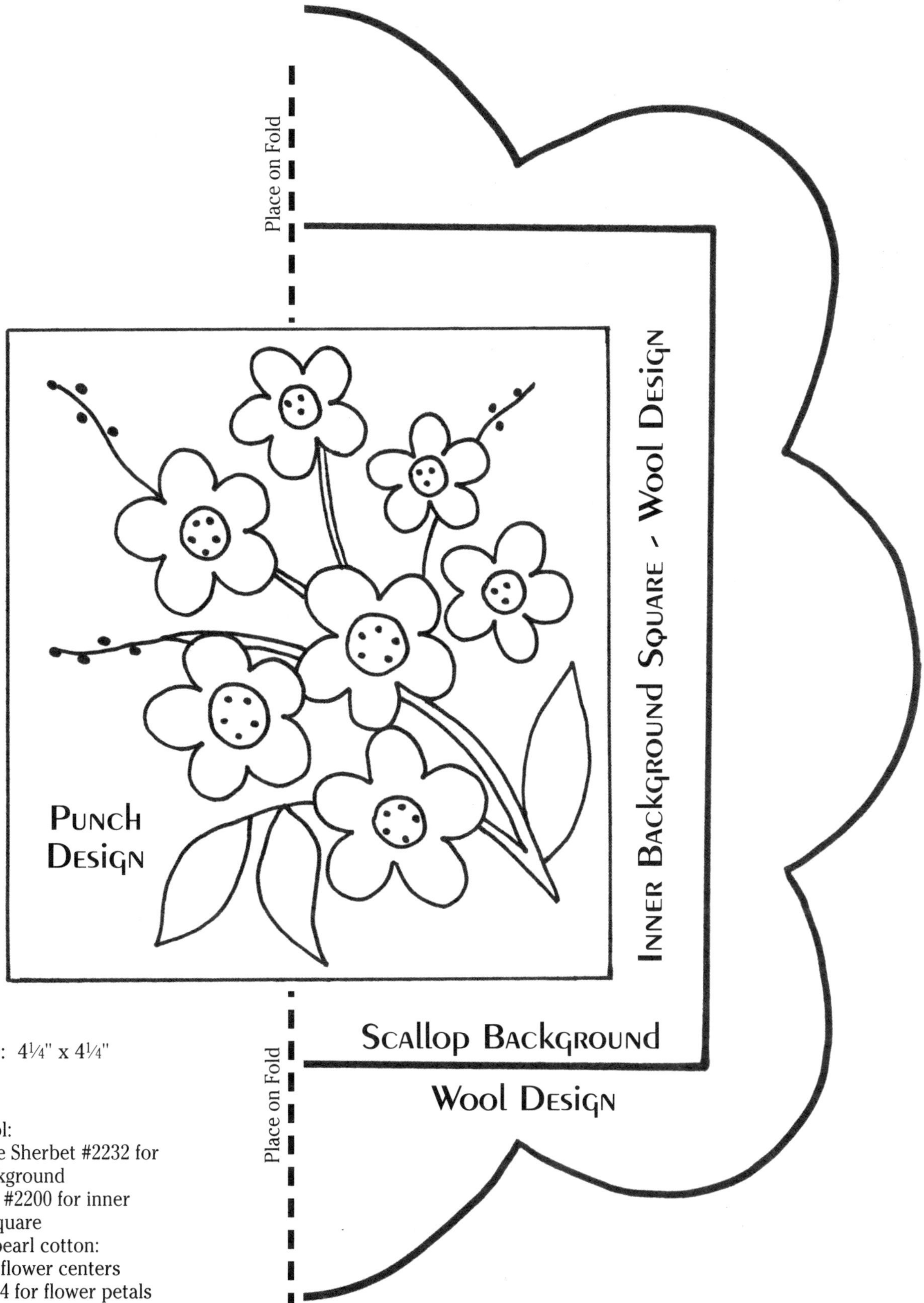

Bouquet of Flowers Mug Rug

photo on page 9

SIZE: Punch needle: 4¼" x 4¼"
8½" x 8½"

MATERIALS:

Weeks Dye Works wool:
- 8½" x 8½" Orange Sherbet #2232 for scalloped background
- 5½" x 5½" Kudzu #2200 for inner background square

Weeks Dye Works #5 pearl cotton:
- Saffron #2223 for flower centers
- 2 Lemonade #1114 for flower petals
- Sage #1191 for leaves
- 4 Navy Blue #1306 for background and French Knots

DMC #8 pearl cotton, Olive #580 for Blanket stitching around backgrounds

7" x 7" Weaver's cloth

INSTRUCTIONS:

Punch in the following order: Flower centers • Flower petals • Leaves • Background

Make Navy Blue French Knots on the centers of each flower.

See page 19 for Finishing instructions.

1. Cut scalloped background from pattern. Blanket stitch around with Olive pearl cotton.
2. Blanket stitch Kudzu square to center of scalloped background with Olive pearl cotton.
3. Whipstitch the finished punch needle project to the center.

Leaf Wreath Box

photo on page 12

SIZE: Punch needle: 4" x 4⅜" - Box: 5" x 5" x 2½" tall

MATERIALS:

Weeks Dye Works #5 pearl cotton:
- Molasses #1268 for leaf
- Carrot #2226 for leaf
- Amber #1224 for leaf
- Concord #1318 for leaf
- Brick #1331 for leaf
- 2 Scuppermong #2196 for inner background
- Juniper #2158 for outer background

7" x 8" Weaver's cloth
5" x 5" x 2½" wood box
Hot glue gun

INSTRUCTIONS:

Punch in the following order: Each leaf with Molasses, Carrot, Amber, Concord, and Brick • Inner background • Outer background
See page 19 for Finishing instructions.
Hot glue finished project to the wood box.

Leaf Wreath Pillow

photo on page 12

SIZE: 12½" x 12½"

MATERIALS:

National Nonwovens wool felt:
- 5" x 6" Leaves (Burgundy, Bright Gold, Light Gold, Rusty Tan, Orange)
- Two 13" x 13" Green for pillow front and back

DMC #8 pearl cotton Gold #783
Poly-fil stuffing

INSTRUCTIONS:

1. Cut out leaves and position on pillow front. Whipstitch in place.
2. Sew a Running stitch down the center and veins of each leaf using Gold pearl cotton.
3. With right sides together, sew a ¼" seam all the way around, leaving 6" open for turning.
4. Turn right side out. Stuff with Poly-fil and hand stitch the opening closed.
5. Blanket stitch all the way around the seam using the Gold pearl cotton.

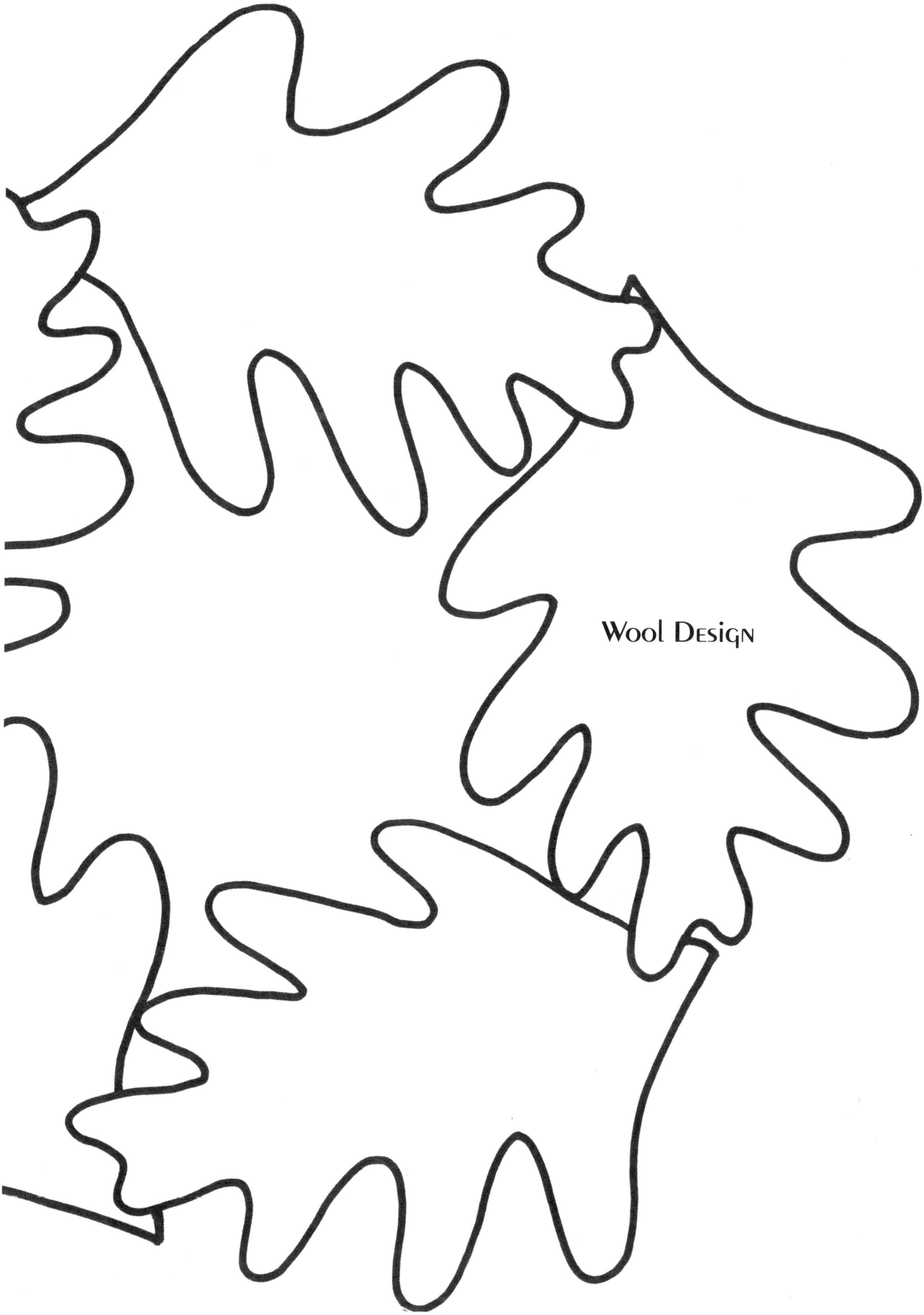
Wool Design

Punch Design

Give Thanks

photo on page 14
SIZE: Punch needle: 3½" x 3¾"
Frame: 5" x 7"

MATERIALS:

Weeks Dye Works #5 pearl cotton:
- Fawn #1111 for faces
- Whiskey #2219 for hair
- Whitewash #1091 for hats and collars
- Terra Cotta #2239 for letters
- Charcoal #1303 for mouths and background

7" x 7" Weaver's cloth
5" x 7" *Weeks Dye Works* Burnt Orange wool for framing
5" x 7" frame
Fabric glue

INSTRUCTIONS:

Punch in the following order: Mouths • Faces • Hair • Collars and hats • Letters • Background
Make French Knots for the eyes with Dark Brown.
Adhere Burnt Orange wool to frame mat.
Glue finished punch needle piece to center of frame.

Give Thanks Wool Pillow

photo on page 14
SIZE: 12" x 12"

MATERIALS:

National Nonwovens wool felt:
- Two 12" x 12" Chocolate for pillow front and back
- 2" x 4" Wheat fields for faces
- 5" x 6" White for bonnets and collars
- 2" x 4" Smoke for man's hat
- 2" x 12" Polynesian Sunset for letters
- 2" x 3" Light Brown for hair

#8 pearl cotton (Black, White, Gold)
Steam-A-Seam II fusible web
Craft & Applique Sheet

INSTRUCTIONS:

1. Following manufacturer's instructions, trace patterns in reverse onto fusible web paper.
2. Cut apart and press to the back of wool felt.
3. Cut out each piece.
4. Position each figure over the pattern on the Craft & Applique Sheet.
5. Fuse pieces together. Cool.
6. Peel off the Craft & Applique Sheet and position on pillow front.
7. Position the words on the pillow top.
8. Fuse all the pieces in place.
9. Using Black pearl cotton, sew French Knots for the eyes and Satin stitch the eyebrows.
10. Sew a Running stitch around hats and collars.
11. With right sides together, sew the pillow with a ¼" seam, leaving 6" open for turning.
12. Turn right side out. Stuff with Poly-fil and hand-stitch the opening closed.
13. Blanket stitch all the way around the seam using Gold pearl cotton.

GIVE
HANKS

Wool Design

Enlarge Pattern to 150%

Holly Leaves Wool Table Runner

photo on page 15

SIZE: 17" x 26"

MATERIALS:

Weeks Dye Works wool:

- 17" x 26" Parchment #1110 for background
- Two 6¼" x 13" Candy Apple HT #2268 for inner border
- Two 5" x 12" Parchment #1110 for inner section
- 10" x 12" Juniper #2158 for leaves
- 3" x 12" Chestnut #1269 for branches
- 2" x 4" Candy Apple #2268 for berries

DMC pearl cotton #5 Beige #738 for sewing around the outer edge of the runner

INSTRUCTIONS:

1. Cut out all of the pieces.
2. Whipstitch Red and Parchment backgrounds on each end of runner.
3. Position appliques. Whipstitch in place.
4. Blanket stitch around the outer edges.

Holly Twig Mug Rug

photo on page 15

SIZE: Punch Needle: 2¼" x 5"
Mug Rug: 8½" x 11¼"

MATERIALS:

Weeks Dye Works wool:

- 8½" x 11½" Candy Apple #2268 for background
- 6½" x 9¼" Camel #1220 for inner background
- 1" x 3" Candy Apple #2268 for berries
- 2" x 4" Brown for stem
- 3" x 8" Green for leaves

Weeks Dye Works #5 pearl cotton:

- Turkish Red #2266 for berries
- Mocha #1236 for stem
- Blue Spruce #1276 for leaves
- 2 Beige #1106 for inner background

DMC #5 pearl cotton

- Bright Red #321 for outer edge of Candy Apple background

5½" x 8" Weaver's cloth

INSTRUCTIONS:

Punch in the following order: Berries • Leaves • Stem • 3 rows of Red inner border •Background

See page 19 for Finishing instructions.

1. Cut out appliques and Whipstitch to Camel background.
2. Blanket stitch the finished punch needle project to the center.
3. Blanket stitch Camel background to Candy Apple background with Beige pearl cotton.
4. Blanket stitch around Candy Apple background with Bright Red pearl cotton.

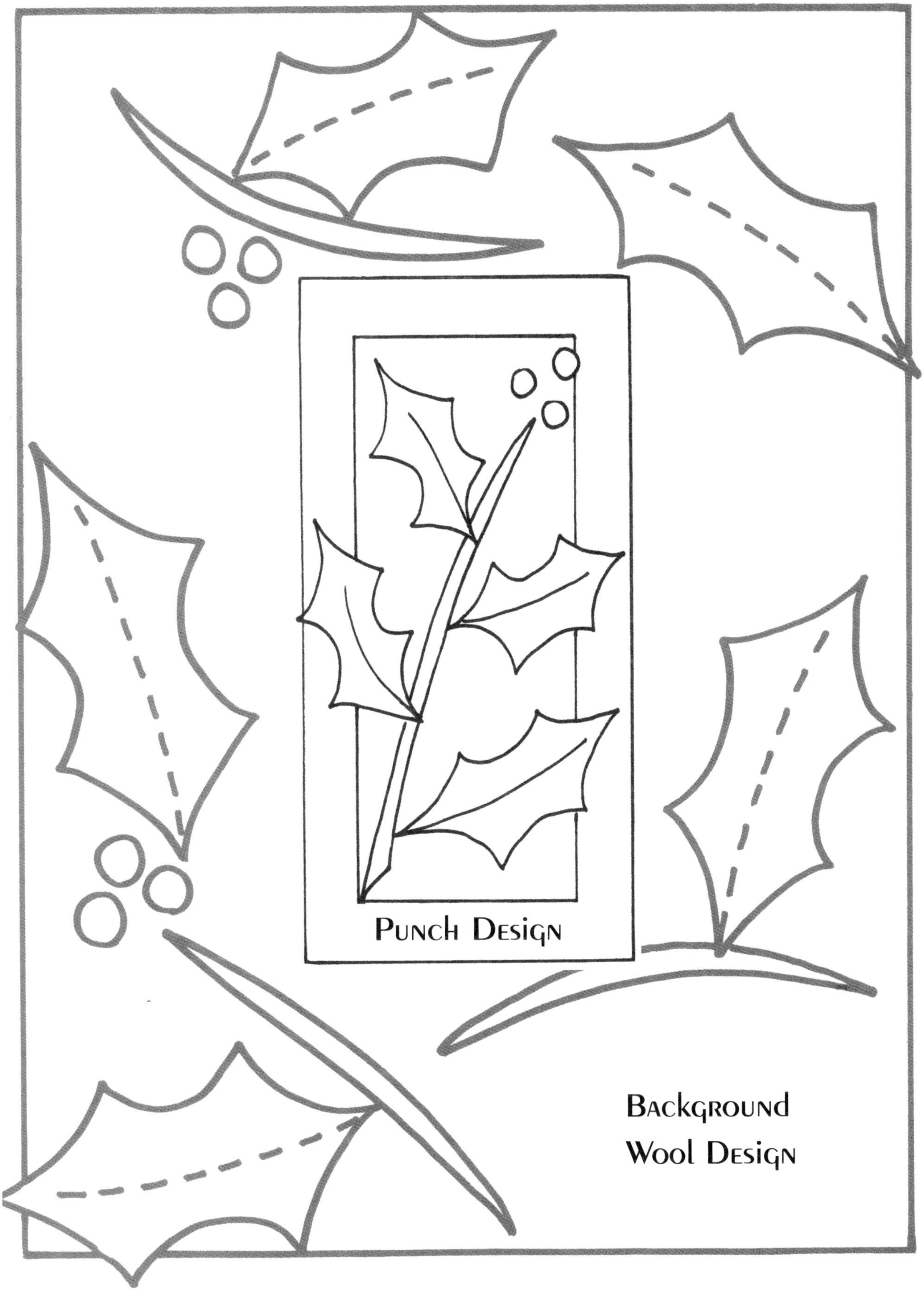

Punch Design
Background
Wool Design

PUNCH DESIGN

Poinsettias

photo on page 16

SIZE: 2¾" x 4⅜"

Frame: 4" x 6"

MATERIALS:

Weeks Dye Works #5 pearl cotton:

- Garnet #2264 for flowers and berries
- Juniper #2158 for pine and leaves
- Whiskey #2219 for bowl
- 3 Light Khaki #1101 for background

6" x 8" Weaver's cloth

3 Gold buttons

4" x 6" *Weeks Dye Works* Red wool for framing

4" x 6" frame

Fabric glue

INSTRUCTIONS:

Punch in the following order: Flowers and berries • Pine and leaves • Bowl • Background

See page 19 for Finishing instructions.

Sew buttons on the center of each flower.

Adhere Red wool to the frame background.

Adhere finished piece to center of frame.

Poinsettia Wool Pillow

photo on page 16

SIZE: 12" x 15"

MATERIALS:

Weeks Dye Works wool:
- Kohl #3900 for 16" x 26" pillow background
- Candy Apple #2268 for flowers and berry
- Collards #1227 for leaves
- Whiskey #2219 for flower pot

DMC #5 pearl cotton:
- Green #935
- Gold #783

White chalk pencil

Poly-fil stuffing

INSTRUCTIONS:

1. Cut out flowers, leaves and vase from wool.
2. Fold the Black wool in half to form the front and back of pillow.
3. Position and pin the pieces in place on the pillow front. Whipstitch using matching thread.
4. Make Gold French Knots on the flowers using Gold pearl cotton.
5. Using a chalk pencil, hand-draw the pine twigs. Stitch twigs using Green pearl cotton.
6. Fold the Black piece in half with the design on the inside.
7. Sew each side and across the bottom, leaving 6" open for turning.
8. Turn right side out. Stuff with Poly-fil. Hand stitch the opening closed.

Cardinal

photo on page 3

SIZE: Punch needle: 3" x 3⅜"

Box: 4" x 4" x 1" tall

MATERIALS:

Crescent Colours 3 strands embroidery floss

- Finley Gold for beak
- Black Coffee for face area
- Desert Mesquite for pine
- LaTierra for stick
- Cupid for wing
- Bandana for bird's body
- 3 Antique Lace for background and French Knot for eye

6" x 7" Weaver's cloth

6" x 6" *Weeks Dye Works* Red wool for covering box lid

4" x 4" x 1" cardboard jewelry box

Hot glue gun

INSTRUCTIONS:

Punch in the following order:

- Beak
- Face area
- Pine • Stick
- Wing
- Bird's body
- Background

Make a small French Knot on the eye area.
See page 19 for Finishing instructions.
Glue Red wool to the box lid.
Glue the finished punch needle project to the center of the lid.

Cardinals Table Runner

photo on page 3

SIZE: 16" x 26"

MATERIALS:

Weeks Dye Works wool:
- 16" x 26" Dove #1171 for table runner background
- 16" x 26" wool for backing
- 12" x 13" Candy Apple #2268 for bird
- 4" x 6" Candy Apple HT #2268 for wing
- 6" x 13" Chestnut #1269 for branch
- 7" x 10" Collards #1227 for pine
- 2" x 2" Mustard #1224 for beak
- 3" x 4" Kohl #3900 for face area

DMC #5 pearl cotton:
- Ecru for French Knot eyes
- Steel Blue #926 for sewing around outer edge of table runner

Wool Design

INSTRUCTIONS:
1. Cut out all the pieces 2 times, 1 for each end.
2. Position all of the pieces on top of the pattern and pin together.
3. Transfer to the Blue wool and pin in place.
4. Whipstitch all the pieces to the wool using matching thread.
5. Make 1 Ecru French Knot on each of the eyes.
6. Lay the runner on a second piece of wool for a backing.
7. Make a Blanket stitch around the outer edges to attach the 2 pieces using matching pearl cotton.

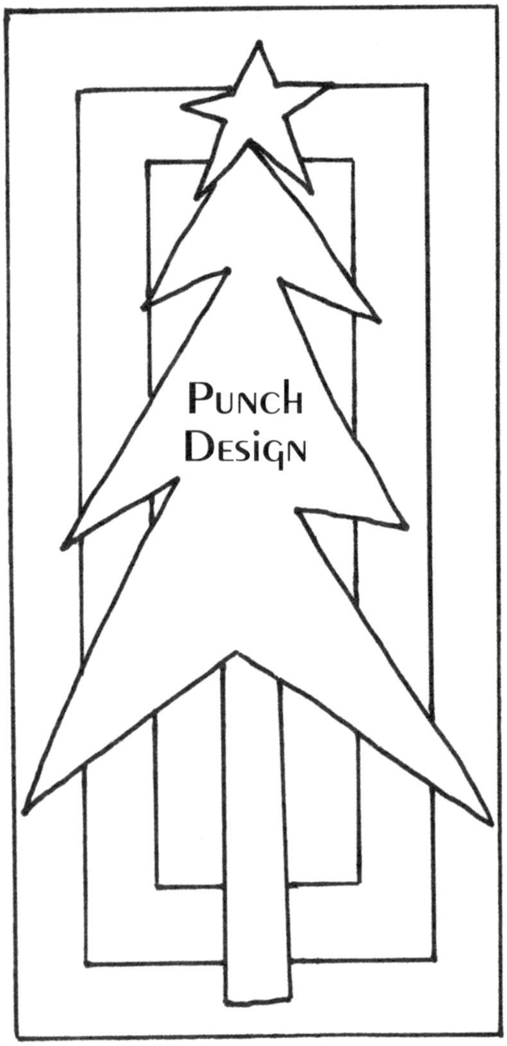

Lonely Tree

photo on page 17

SIZE: Punch needle: 2½" x 5½"
Frame: 5" x 7"

MATERIALS:

Weeks Dye Works #5 pearl cotton:
- Curry #2220 for star
- Hunter #2158 for tree
- Chestnut #1269 for tree trunk
- Putty #1201 for inner background
- Beige #1106 for middle background
- 2 Angel Hair #1109 for outer background

6" x 10" Weaver's cloth
5" x 7" *Weeks Dye Works* Green wool for framing
5" x 7" frame
Fabric glue

INSTRUCTIONS:

Punch in the following order: Star • Tree • Tree trunk • Inner background• Middle background • Outer background

See page 19 for Finishing instructions.

Adhere Green wool to matboard in the frame.
Adhere project to wool with fabric glue.

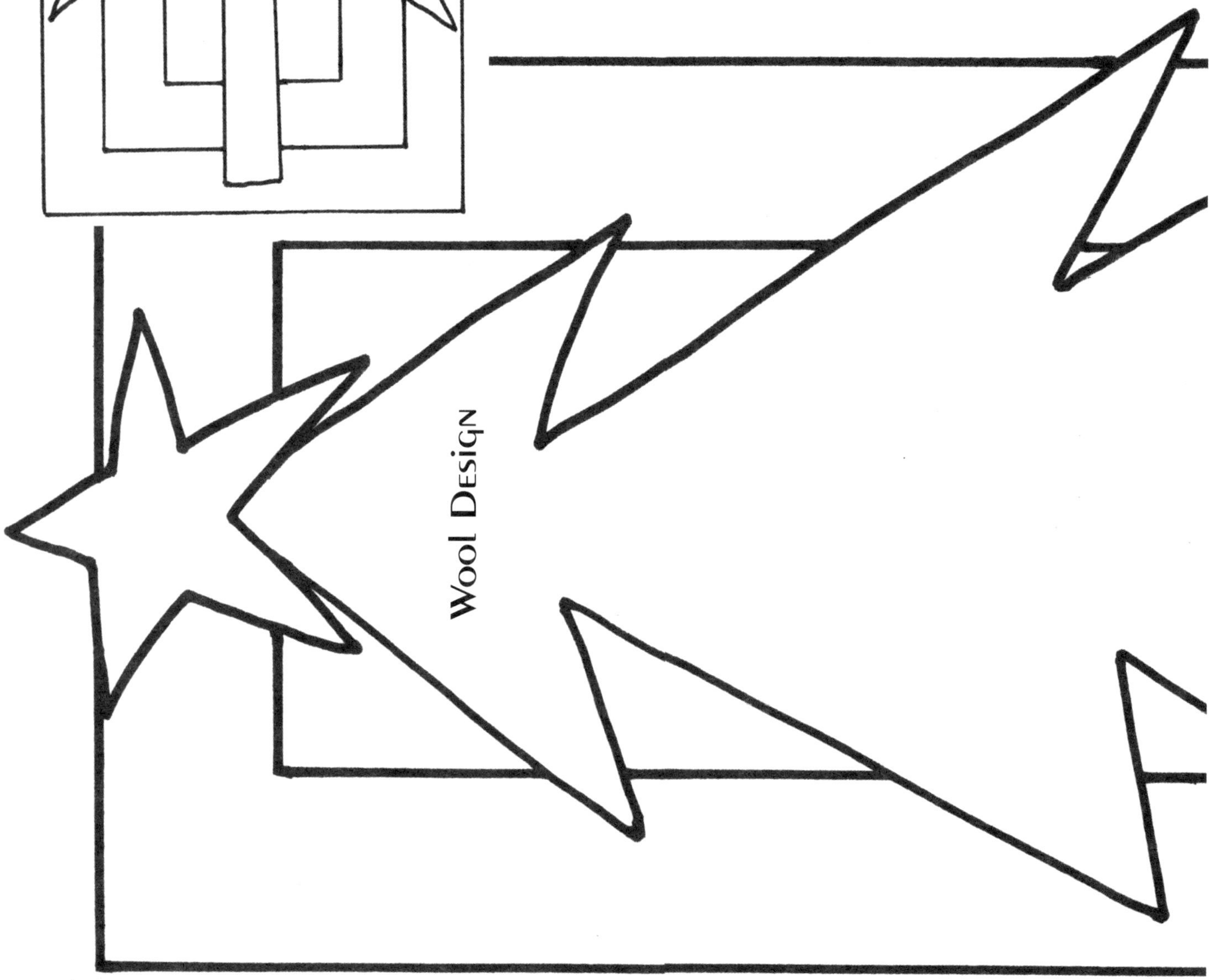

Lonely Tree Wool Table Mat

photo on page 17

SIZE: 8" x 15½"

MATERIALS:

Weeks Dye Works hand-dyed wool:

- 7½" x 12" Juniper #2158 for tree
- 1¼" x 6" Chestnut #1269 for trunk
- 3" x 3" Mustard #1227 for star
- Two 8" x 15½" Beige for background and backing
- 5½" x 12¾" Brown Houndstooth for middle layer
- 3¼" x 10¾" Tan behind the tree
- Two 1" x 4" strips Beige for hanging loops

INSTRUCTIONS:

1. Position the Brown and Tan layers on Beige background. Blanket stitch in place.
2. Cut out the tree, trunk and star.
3. Position appliques and Whipstitch in place using matching thread.
4. With wrong sides together, layer appliqued top and backing.
5. Blanket stitch around the outer edge using matching pearl cotton.
6. Fold the hanging loops in half and Whipstitch the back side.

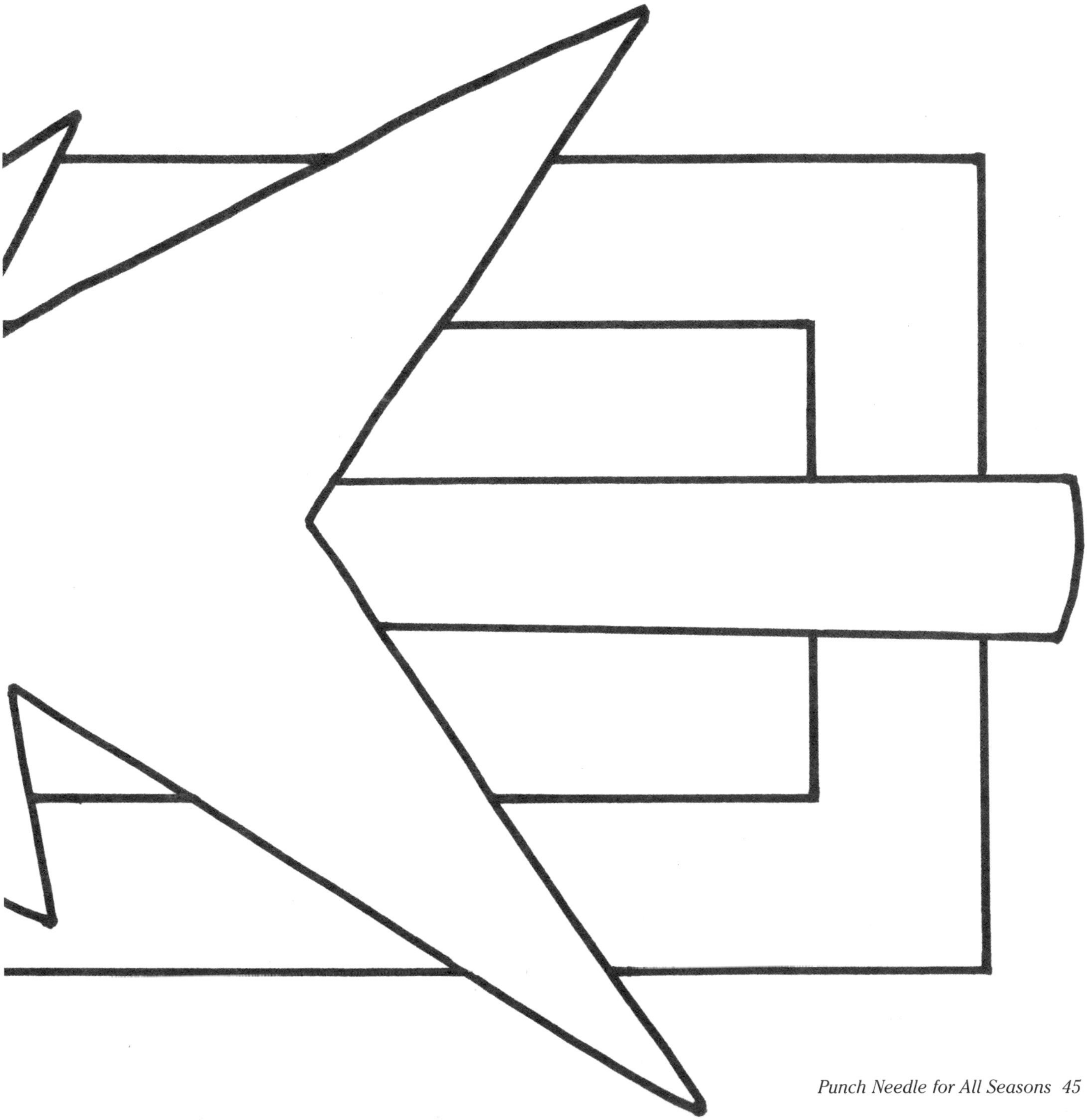

Jar Lid Information

photo on page 18
SIZE: 3" diameter
GENERAL MATERIALS:
7" x 7" Weaver's cloth
3" diameter jar lid
Craft & Applique Sheet
Fabric glue • Hot glue gun

GENERAL INSTRUCTIONS:
If your lid has 2 pieces, you must connect them together before adding the punch needle project. If desired, punch a hole in each side for adding string to hang. • Punch a design. • Trace the jar lid onto the back of the work.
Coat the back of the fabric with fabric glue.
Lay flat on a Craft & Applique sheet to dry overnight.
Peel off the sheet and cut around the circle very close with scissors.
Adhere finished piece to lid with hot glue.

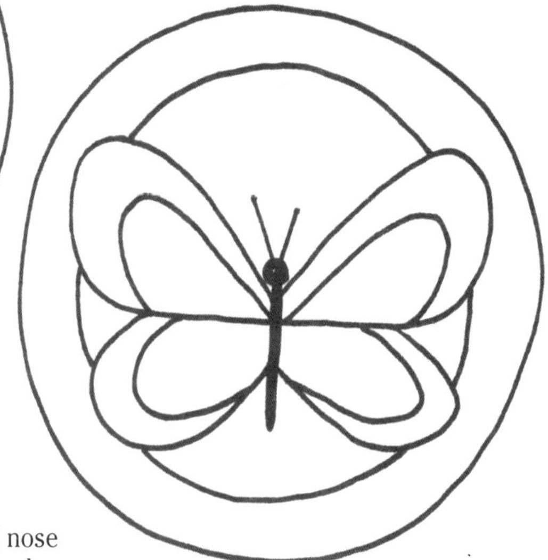

Butterfly

MATERIALS:
Weeks Dye Works #8 pearl cotton:
- Onyx #1304 for body
- MariGold #2225 for inner wings
- Carrot #2226 for outer wings
- Navy #1306 for outer background

DMC #8 pearl cotton:
- Light Blue #800 for inner background

INSTRUCTIONS:
Punch in the following order:
Body • Inner wings • Outer wings • Inner background • Outer background

Bunny

MATERIALS:
Weeks Dye Works #8 pearl cotton:
- Sweetheart Rose #2279 for heart and nose
- Morris Blue #2109 for inner background
- Sky #2111 for outer background

DMC #8 pearl cotton:
- Ecru for bunny
- Black or Brown for eye

INSTRUCTIONS:
Punch in the following order: Heart and nose • Bunny • Inner background • Outer background
Make 1 French Knot on the eye using Black or Brown.

Punch Design

Pumpkin Wood Box

photo on page 13
SIZE: Punch needle: 2⅞" x 3¼"
Box: 3" wide x 4" long x 2" tall
MATERIALS:
DMC 3 strands floss:
- Dark Yellow #3821 for flowers
- Light Yellow #744 for flowers
- Brown #938 for French Knots and stem
- Green #3051 for leaves
- Light Orange #922 for center of pumpkin
- Medium Orange #3776 for sides of pumpkin
- Dark Orange #918 for Dark outer edge of pumpkin
- 2 Ecru for background

6" x 6" Weaver's cloth
3" x 4" x 2" wooden box
Hot glue gun
INSTRUCTIONS:
Punch in the following order: 2 Dark Yellow flowers • 3 Light Yellow flowers • Center of pumpkin • Outline the center with Dark Orange • Back pumpkin with Dark Orange • Middle section of pumpkin with medium Orange • Stem • Leaves • Background
Make French Knots in the center of flowers with Brown.
See page 19 for Finishing instructions.
Hot glue to wooden box.

Cat

MATERIALS:
Weeks Dye Works #8 pearl cotton:
MariGold #2225 for cat body
Navy #2104 for background
Black for eye and mouth
INSTRUCTIONS:
Punch in the following order: Cat body • Background
Make a French Knot for the eyes. Make a Satin stitch across the mouth.

Holiday Wreath

MATERIALS:
DMC #8 pearl cotton:
Berry Red #321 for berries and border
Forest Green #890
Hunter Green #3345 for alternating leaves
Sand #739 for background
INSTRUCTIONS:
Punch in the following order: Berries • Leaves alternating with Hunter Green and Forest Green Background • 1 Red row around the border

Bottle Cap Information

photo on page 2 SIZE: $1\frac{3}{8}$" diameter
GENERAL MATERIALS:
$4\frac{1}{2}$" x $4\frac{1}{2}$" Weaver's cloth, Bottle cap
Craft & Applique Sheet, Fabric glue, Hot glue gun
GENERAL INSTRUCTIONS:
Flatten bottle cap. • Punch a design.
Trace bottle cap onto the back of work.
Coat the back of the fabric with fabric glue.
Lay flat on a Craft & Applique sheet to dry overnight.
Peel off the sheet and cut around the circle very close with scissors. • Punch a hole in the bottle cap and insert a string for hanging.
Adhere finished piece to bottle cap with hot glue.

Cardinal Bottle Cap

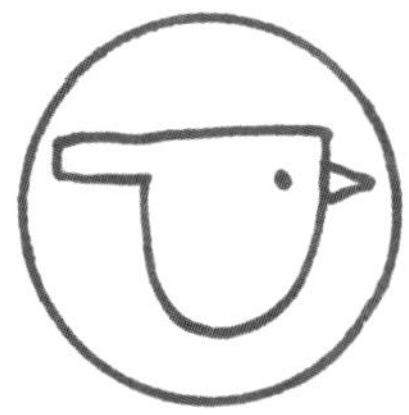

MATERIALS:
Weeks Dye Works #8 pearl cotton:
Liberty #2269 for bird
Onyx #1304 for background and eye
DMC #8 pearl cotton Gold #783 for beak
INSTRUCTIONS:
Punch in the following order: • Beak • Body • Background
Make a French Knot on the eye.

Heart Bottle Cap

MATERIALS:
Weeks Dye Works #8 pearl cotton:
Sweetheart Rose #2279 for heart
Beige #1106 for background
INSTRUCTIONS:
Punch in the following order: • Heart • Background

Daisy Bottle Cap

MATERIALS:
Weeks Dye Works #8 pearl cotton:
Lemonade #1114 for flower petals
Onyx #1304 for center of flower
Scuppermong #2196 for background
INSTRUCTIONS:
Punch in the following order: Center of flower • Flower petals • Background

Star Bottle Cap

MATERIALS:
Weeks Dye Works #8 pearl cotton:
Whiskey #2219 for star
Deep Sea #2104 for background
INSTRUCTIONS:
Punch in the following order: • Star • Background

Holly Bottle Cap

MATERIALS:
Weeks Dye Works #8 pearl cotton:
Liberty #2269 for berries
Hunter #2156 for holly
Beige #1106 for background
INSTRUCTIONS:
Punch in the following order: • Berries • Holly • Background

Pumpkins Table Runner

photo on page 13

SIZE: 16" x 26"

MATERIALS:

Weeks Dye Works wool:

- 16" x 26" Kohl #3900 for background
- 4" x 5" Terra Cotta #2239 Orange for center of pumpkin
- 4" x 8" Terra Cotta #2239 HT medium Orange for middle pumpkin
- 5" x 8" Terra Cotta #2239 HB Darkest Orange for bottom pumpkin
- 10" x 10" Mustard #1227 for Gold flowers
- 8" x 8" Juniper #2158 for leaves
- 1" x 2" Palomino #1232 for stem

National Nonwovens wool felt:

- 16" x 26" Black for backing

#5 pearl cotton:

- Orange for sewing around outside of runner
- Brown for French Knots

INSTRUCTIONS:

1. Cut 2 of all the pieces, 1 for each end of table runner.
2. Position pieces on top of the pattern and pin together.
3. Transfer to the Black wool and pin in place.
4. Whipstitch pieces to the wool using matching thread.
5. Make 3 Brown French Knots on each of the Gold flowers.
6. Lay the runner on a second piece of Black wool felt backing.
7. Blanket stitch around the outer edges using Orange pearl cotton.

Snowman Wool Table Runner

photo on page 51
instructions on page 50

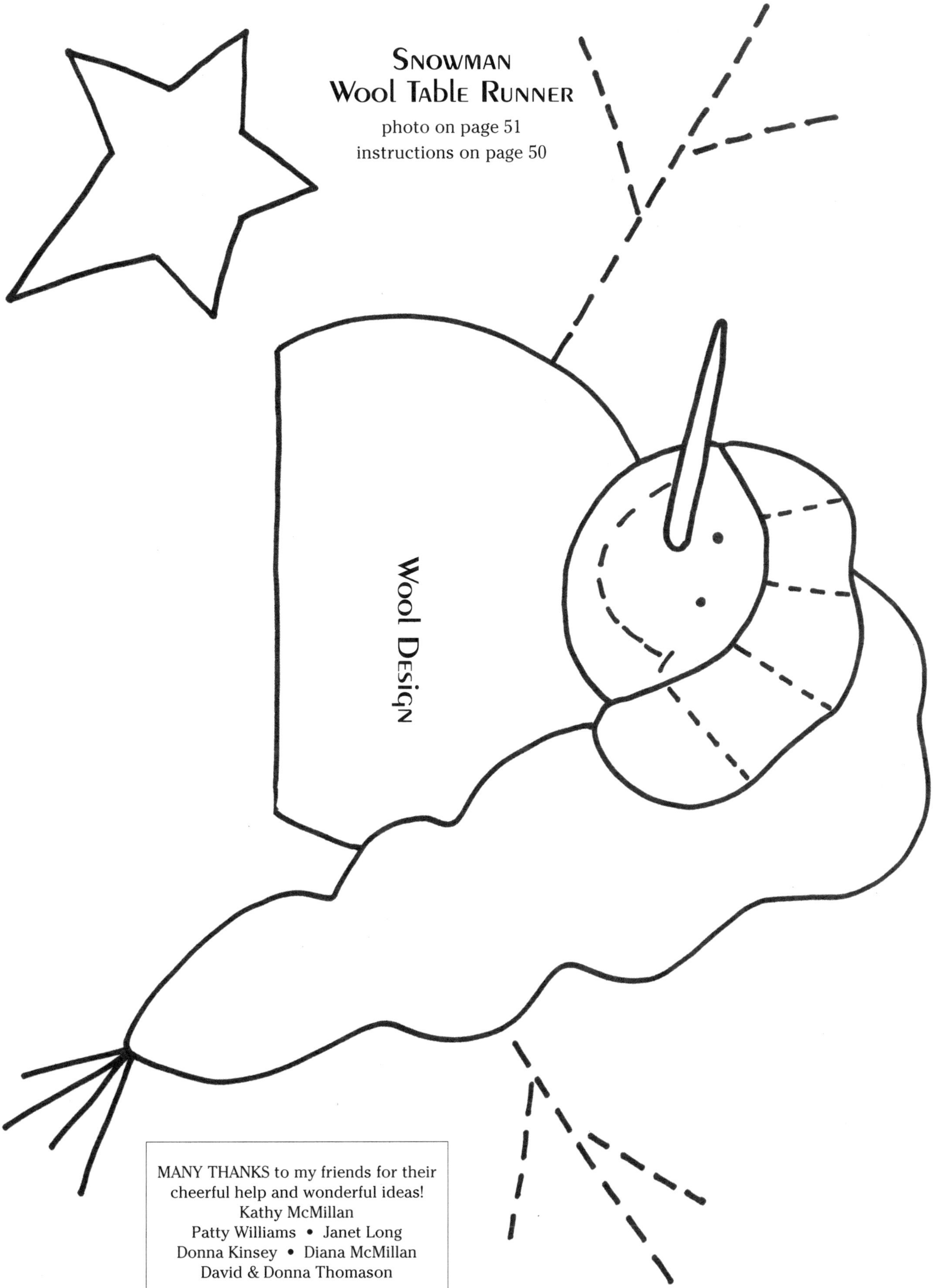

MANY THANKS to my friends for their cheerful help and wonderful ideas!
Kathy McMillan
Patty Williams • Janet Long
Donna Kinsey • Diana McMillan
David & Donna Thomason

Snowman Box

photo on page 51

SIZE: Punch needle: $3\frac{3}{4}$" x $4\frac{1}{4}$"
Box: $5\frac{1}{2}$" wide x $5\frac{1}{2}$" long x $2\frac{1}{4}$" tall

MATERIALS:

DMC #5 pearl cotton:
- Orange #900 for nose
- Tan #842 for arms
- Black #310 for French Knots

Weeks Dye Works #5 pearl cotton:
- Turkish Red#2266 for hat and heart
- Whitewash #1091 for body
- Gold #2221 for hat and star
- TwiLight #1285 for background

7" x 7" Weaver's cloth
$5\frac{1}{2}$" x $5\frac{1}{2}$" x $2\frac{1}{4}$" paper mache box
Gold paint, Paintbrush, Hot glue gun

INSTRUCTIONS:

Punch in the following order: Nose • Heart and red parts of hat • Body • Arms • Star and gold parts of hat • Background
Make French Knots on the chest and eyes.
Tie a Gold bow around the hand holding the star.
See page 19 for Finishing instructions.
Paint a paper mache box Gold. Let dry.
Hot glue the finished punch needle project to the center of the box.

Snowman Wool Table Runner

photo on page 51
pattern on page 49

SIZE: 14" x 30"

MATERIALS:

Weeks Dye Works wool:
- Two 4" x 14" Louisiana Hot Sauce HT #2266 for each end of runner
- 4" x 4" Louisiana Hot Sauce #2266 for hat brims
- 6" x 7" Mustard #1224 HB for hats
- 4" x 8" Snow Cream #1096 for body
- 6" x 9" Whiskey #2219 for stars

National Nonwovens wool felt:
- Two 14" x 30" Black
- 1" x 2" Orange for snowman noses

Weeks Dye Works #5 pearl cotton (Gold, Black, Red),
DMC #5 pearl cotton #612 for arms
6 jingle bells • 4 Green buttons
Craft & Applique Sheet
Steam-A-Seam II fusible web

INSTRUCTIONS:

1. Position each 4" x 14" end piece on the Black background. Sew a Running stitch across one long side with Red pearl cotton as shown in photo. Following manufacturer's instructions, trace the patterns in reverse onto fusible web paper.
2. Cut apart and press to the back of wool. Cut out each piece.
3. Position each snowman over the pattern on the Craft & Applique Sheet.
4. Press to attach the pieces. Cool.
5. Peel off the Craft & Applique Sheet and position on each end of the runner.
6. Fuse all the pieces in place.
7. Make French Knots for the eyes using Black pearl cotton.
8. Form mouths with small Running stitches.
9. Make a Running stitch across the hat brim using Gold pearl cotton.
10. Make a Running stitch for the arms using #612 pearl cotton.
11. Make 5 stitches from the tip of each hat using Gold pearl cotton.
12. With wrong sides together, layer appliqued top and backing wool.
13. Blanket stitch all the way around using Red pearl cotton.
14. Sew buttons and bells in place.

We thank Barbara Cooley for all her help. Also, many thanks to:

Weeks Dye Works for supplying their beautiful hand-dyed wools, embroidery floss and pearl cottons.

DMC for supplying their embroidery floss, Medicis Wool and pearl cottons.

Just Another Button Company for supplying the sweet handmade buttons. For more great Punch Needle & Wool Embroidery projects, visit online at

www.prairiegrovepeddler.com.

Suppliers - Most craft and variety stores carry an excellent assortment of supplies If you need something special, ask your local store to contact the following companies:

Punch Needle Patterns & Craft & Applique Sheet
Prairie Grove Peddler

Punch Needle Suppliers
Cameo - Punch Needle Marketplace
Birdhouse Enterprises
Norden Crafts
CTR Inc.

Hand-Dyed Wool
Weeks Dye Works

Pearl Cotton
Weeks Dye Works
Crescent Colours
DMC

Steam a Seam II Fusible Web
The Warm Company

Hand Made Buttons
Just Another Button Company

Wool Felt
National Nonwovens

Gripper Frame
Woolen Whimsies